SUPERBIKES

Big Buddy BOOKS
Amazing Vehicles

ABDO
Publishing Company

Sarah Tieck

Amazing Vehicles

VISIT US AT
www.abdopublishing.com

Published by ABDO Publishing Company, 8000 West 78th Street, Edina, Minnesota 55439.

Printed in the United States of America, North Mankato, Minnesota.
102010
012011

 PRINTED ON RECYCLED PAPER

Coordinating Series Editor: Rochelle Baltzer
Contributing Editors: Megan M. Gunderson, BreAnn Rumsch, Marcia Zappa
Graphic Design: Deb Coldiron, Maria Hosley, Marcia Zappa
Cover Photograph: *Shutterstock*: Nildo Scoop.
Interior Photographs/Illustrations: *AP Photo*: AP Photo (p. 29), Bernat Armangue (p. 17), Fernando Bustamante (p. 7), Petr David Josek (p. 25), Press Association via AP Images (p. 27), Tom Riles, AMA Pro Racing, ho (p. 30), Alberto Saiz (p. 13), Steve C. Wilson (p. 25); *Getty Images*: Robert Cianflone (p. 19), Robert Cianflone/Allsport (p. 8), VINCENT JANNINK/AFP (p. 19), Mirco Lazzari (p. 21), Bryn Lennon (p. 5), Adhil Rangel/Latin Content (p. 11), Mark Thompson (p. 13), ANDREW YATES/AFP (p. 29); *Shutterstock*: Nildo Scoop (pp. 10, 14, 22, 25, 28), testing (pp. 15, 23).

Library of Congress Cataloging-in-Publication Data

Tieck, Sarah, 1976-
  Superbikes / Sarah Tieck.
    p. cm.
  ISBN 978-1-61714-700-5
  1. Superbikes--Juvenile literature. 2. Motorcycle racing--Juvenile literature. I. Title.
  TL440.15.T54 2011
  629.227'5--dc22
                      2010029677

CONTENTS

GET MOVING

Imagine riding on a superbike. You tuck your legs behind you and lean forward. Wind rushes past you. As the superbike moves faster, you hear the engine roar.

Have you ever looked closely at a superbike? Many parts work together to make it move. A superbike is an amazing vehicle!

Sometimes, people use the word *superbike* to describe any powerful, fast motorcycle. But, a superbike is a certain type of racing motorcycle.

Superbikes come in different colors and styles. This helps riders stand out!

WHAT IS A SUPERBIKE?

A superbike is a type of motorcycle. It is made for riding very fast on racetracks.

A superbike's shape helps it move quickly along a track. Its slim, rounded body cuts through the wind.

A CLOSER LOOK

A superbike's body is built on a strong frame. This frame holds the superbike's parts.

A superbike has many of the same parts as a standard motorcycle. But, these parts have been **modified** for racing.

SUPERBIKES

1 Handlebars help steer a superbike. Hand controls for the engine and front brakes are connected to the handlebars.

2 To let the bike move faster, a superbike's **engine** is underneath a protective covering.

3 Superbike riders balance on the **seat**. The seat is tilted forward so riders can lean in close to the superbike.

4 A superbike's **fuel tank** is set high in front of the seat. That way, the rider's knees can tuck in close to the superbike.

5 Superbikes have different types of **tires** for different racing conditions. Smooth tires are for dry tracks. Tires with a raised pattern are for wet tracks.

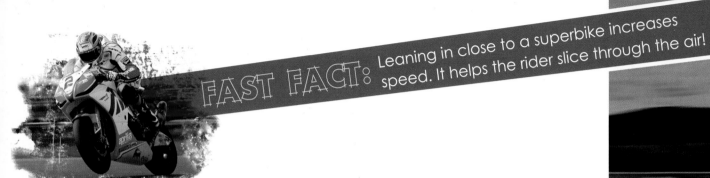

FAST FACT: Leaning in close to a superbike increases speed. It helps the rider slice through the air!

HOW DOES IT MOVE?

Like other motorcycles, a superbike moves when its two wheels turn. But, the wheels need power to move!

The superbike's engine supplies that power. It provides enough force to turn an **axle**. This axle is connected to the superbike's back wheel. When it turns, the wheels turn.

Riders sit with their feet behind them. So, they can get low and close to the ground. This improves their control of the superbike.

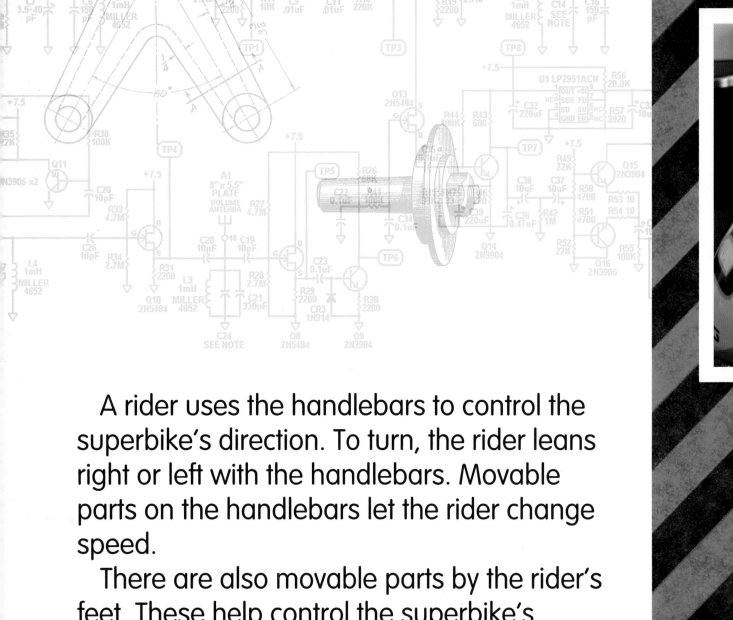

A rider uses the handlebars to control the superbike's direction. To turn, the rider leans right or left with the handlebars. Movable parts on the handlebars let the rider change speed.

There are also movable parts by the rider's feet. These help control the superbike's engine and rear brake.

The handlebars stick out from behind a plastic screen. The screen is shaped to help the superbike cut through the wind.

A rider's knee may touch the ground while going around curves! So, riders wear knee sliders for protection.

POWERFUL ENGINES

Superbikes have powerful engines. An engine's size can be measured in cubic centimeters (cc). Most superbike engines measure about 750 to 1200 cc. A higher number means more power.

Superbike engines have one to four cylinders. A cylinder is the part of the engine where fuel burns, creating power.

People use sportbikes (*right*) on city streets for fun and for transportation.

Superbikes look like sportbikes. However, superbikes are sportbikes that have been **modified**. People add racing parts to build superbikes. This makes them faster and more powerful.

THE DRIVER'S SEAT

Superbikes are fun! But, they can also be unsafe. It takes practice and skill to ride them safely.

Only racers ride superbikes. They have special driver's **licenses**. And, most are **professionals** who are trained to handle the speed and the moves.

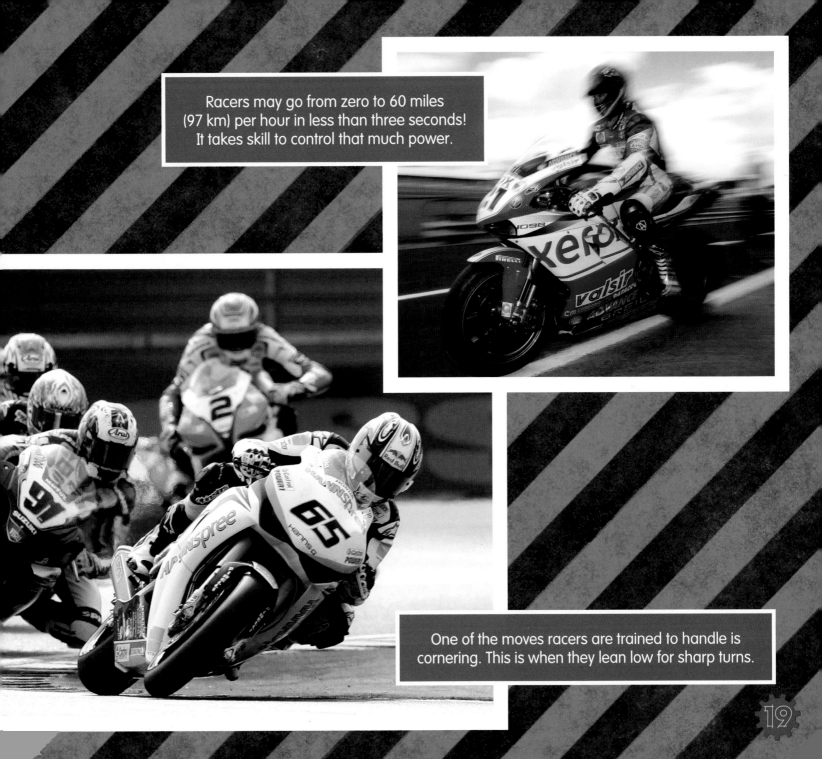

Racers may go from zero to 60 miles (97 km) per hour in less than three seconds! It takes skill to control that much power.

One of the moves racers are trained to handle is cornering. This is when they lean low for sharp turns.

19

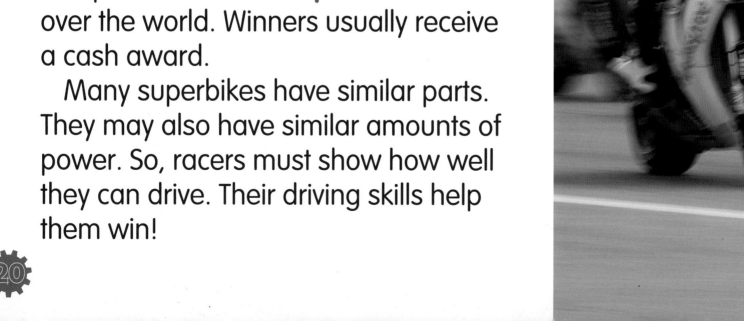

SPEED RACER

Superbike riders **compete** in races all over the world. Winners usually receive a cash award.

Many superbikes have similar parts. They may also have similar amounts of power. So, racers must show how well they can drive. Their driving skills help them win!

During superbike events, riders race at high speeds around **paved** tracks. There are many things that make a superbike go faster. The shape of the windshield and the rider's helmet can help cut through the air. Even a rider's weight can affect speed.

A superbike may have different sizes of tires. The tires can affect a superbike's speed.

NOT JUST FOR LOOKS

Superbikes offer little **protection** for riders. If a superbike's tire slips, the rider may crash. So, wearing special clothing is very important for a racer's safety.

Thick leather suits cover the skin. The parts that cover knees, hips, and elbows are extra thick. Racers wear full face helmets, too. This protects the head, face, and jaw.

Racers often have sponsor names on their clothes and superbikes. Sponsors pay racing costs to gain attention from the public.

FAST FACT: Racing clothes can be hot! So, racing helmets have air slots. These keep racers a little cooler.

25

COOL STUNTS

Some riders do **stunts** and tricks with their superbikes. Sometimes, they put on special shows. Some do wheelies, ride one-handed, or stand on their handlebars!

When a racer's two wheels leave
the ground, it is called "catching air."

PAST TO PRESENT

The first motorcycles had engines powered by steam. They went just ten miles (16 km) per hour! By the 1950s, motorcycles went as fast as cars.

Still, people wanted faster motorcycles. So by the 1960s and the 1970s, companies had created superbikes.

Today, there are many types of motorcycles. Superbikes are some of the fastest and most powerful. Superbikes are amazing vehicles!

Superbike parts have changed and improved over the years. But, today's racers still use some of the same moves as early racers used.

BLAST FROM THE PAST

Superbike racing is popular around the world. The longest-running **championship** is the American Motorcyclist Association (AMA) Superbike Championship. This U.S. race started in 1976.

There, superbike makers show off their new styles. And, racing teams show their skills. Mat Mladin is one of the most successful AMA Superbike Championship racers. He has won the title seven times!

IMPORTANT WORDS

axle (AK-suhl) a bar on which a wheel or a pair of wheels turns.

championship a game, a match, or a race held to find a first-place winner.

compete to take part in a contest between two or more persons or groups.

license (LEYE-suhnts) a paper or a card showing that someone is allowed to do something by law.

modify to change something from the original.

pave to cover with a material, such as tar, to make a level surface for travel.

professional (pruh-FEHSH-nuhl) working for money rather than for pleasure.

protection (pruh-TEHK-shuhn) the act of protecting, or guarding against harm or danger.

stunt an action requiring great skill or daring.

WEB SITES

To learn more about superbikes, visit ABDO Publishing Company online. Web sites about superbikes are featured on our Book Links page. These links are routinely monitored and updated to provide the most current information available.

www.abdopublishing.com

INDEX